by Cass Evans
illustrated by Ron Berg

Harcourt
SCHOOL PUBLISHERS

Printed in China

ISBN 10: 0-15-351507-4
ISBN 13: 978-0-15-351507-1

Ordering Options
ISBN 10: 0-15-351213-X (Grade 3 Advanced Collection)
ISBN 13: 978-0-15-351213-1 (Grade 3 Advanced Collection)
ISBN 10: 0-15-358097-6 (package of 5)
ISBN 13: 978-0-15-358097-0 (package of 5)

4 5 6 7 8 9 10 0940 12 11 10 09

It is dawn. In a ragged nest far above the ground, two large peregrine falcons stir. They wait for the gray light to brighten. Beside them, three smaller birds become active as well. They are the chicks of the larger pair, and they are very hungry. When they were hatched, they weighed about the same as a golf ball. Now they are four times the size they were when they were born.

The chicks seem interested in almost everything. They move to the edge of the ledge on which this high nest rests. They bob their heads. Their mother pushes them back because they are not ready to fly yet.

The morning light has strengthened. Almost without effort, the mother spreads her wings and takes to the air. The father, a slightly smaller bird, stays to guard the nest. The falcons are active during the day because they are not nocturnal.

The mother is on the hunt for other birds. No detail escapes her keen eyesight. She spies a victim and circles above it once. Then she dives at her target. As she drops from the sky, she goes so fast that she is hard to see. No other bird can match her speed.

She stuns her prey in midair, and then she catches it. She swoops low near the ground and then soars back up again to return to the nest. The eager chicks are glad to see her.

This drama may not have taken place where you think it did. The high nesting ledge is on a skyscraper, more than fifty floors above a busy city street. The capture of the smaller bird took place over the heads of hundreds of people. The young birds were not born on a windy cliff, but in New York City, one of the busiest cities in the world.

Just a short while ago, peregrine falcons had almost disappeared. The word *peregrine* comes from the Latin word for wandering. These birds are an unusual success story because thousands of people have the opportunity to observe them since they live in the city. Not many recovering species have such a large audience.

Later in the morning, the father peregrine flies around the city. In normal flight, he will fly at speeds of up to 55 miles (88 km) per hour. When he dives, he may reach speeds of over 200 miles (321 km) per hour! Peregrine falcons have been called the fastest living things on earth.

Peregrine falcons almost always lived on high cliffs in the past. They could launch their amazing dives from these high cliffs. Long before humans built cities, peregrine falcons were nesting on rocky mountainsides.

Humans, though, almost destroyed these birds. A chemical called DDT was sprayed on crops to kill insects. Unfortunately, the DDT in the air and the water hurt the falcons. It made their eggs so thin that the eggs broke when the falcons sat on them to hatch. By the early 1960s, there were no breeding peregrine falcons left in the eastern United States. That means that there were no falcons that were hatching new chicks. In 1972, the government said that people could no longer use DDT.

People tried to save the falcons. They captured some and raised the baby falcons in captivity. Then people tried releasing them into the wild. It was hard work. The young falcons had to learn to feed themselves. They had to learn to adapt to new places. Because the young birds did not know to avoid owls, raccoons, and foxes in the wild, people tried placing them in cities. It was hoped that the falcons would have a better chance to survive there.

The idea worked. Cities are a good place for the falcons to live. The high buildings and bridges remind the falcons of natural places they once lived. There is plenty of food. Pigeons, starlings, blackbirds, and other city birds are prey for the falcons.

In cities, workers can also keep track of the birds. They do this by banding the falcons. This means that when the falcons are babies, scientists put bands on their legs. Each band has different letters and numbers on it. That way the scientists can tell which bird is which.

Scientists climb up on bridges, skyscrapers, and other difficult places to reach, in order to band the young birds. It is a dangerous job because the falcons do not like their nests to be disturbed. High on a bridge girder or on a skyscraper ledge is not an easy place to deal with an angry peregrine falcon.

The young are banded at about four weeks of age. By then, their feet will not grow much more. They are checked carefully, and then returned to their nest.

Peregrine falcons usually lay three to five eggs that hatch in about four weeks. For the first day or so, the babies do not need to eat. Then they eat meat gently provided by their parents. Both male and female peregrines help care for the young.

When the chicks are born, they are covered with soft down. Then, when they are about three weeks old, their flight feathers come in. The young birds are soon fluttering their wings at the edge of their nests. At about six or seven weeks of age, they fly. By twelve weeks, they can feed themselves.

New Yorkers often stop to watch the amazing flights of the peregrines. It is important for observers not to disturb the birds' nests, feed them, or try to tame them. They must remain wild. That is why the city of New York does not release the locations of the peregrines' nests.

Late in the afternoon, the father dozes in the warm sun on the ledge. He will probably hunt once more before nightfall. He does not know how close his kind came to being gone forever.

Think Critically

1. How are the falcons' new homes in cities similar to their previous homes in high cliffs and mountainsides?

2. How might banding the birds help people learn more about them?

3. How did DDT cause problems for falcons?

4. Why are young falcons safer in cities than they might be in the wild?

5. Why doesn't the city of New York release the exact locations of falcon nests?

 Science

Bird Facts Find out about another large bird of prey, such as an eagle, in a science book or on the Internet. Write three facts that you found about the bird.

School-Home Connection What birds live in your neighborhood? With family members or friends, make a list of as many birds as you can that you have observed in your area.

Word Count: 988